# THE KREGEL PICTORIAL GUIDE TO CHURCH HISTORY

## VOLUME 6—THE CHURCH AND POSTMODERNITY
## A.D. 1900–PRESENT

JOHN D. HANNAH

Kregel Publications

*The Kregel Pictorial Guide to Church History, Volume 6* by John D. Hannah



Published by Kregel Publications, a division of Kregel, Inc., PO Box 2607, Grand Rapids, MI 49501.

ISBN 978-0-8254-2787-9



Worldwide coedition produced by
Lion Hudson plc
Wilkinson House
Jordan Hill Road
Oxford OX2 8DR, England
Tel: +44 (0) 1865 302750
Fax: +44 (0) 1865 302757
E-mail: coed@lionhudson.com
www.lionhudson.com

Printed in China

Picture acknowledgments

**Photographs**
Illustrated London News: pp. 5, 6, 7 left, 29
SCM: pp. 7 right, 9
Zev Radovan: p. 10
Gospel Light: p. 12
Billy Graham Evangelistic Association: pp. 13, 14/15 bottom, 18
Campus Crusade: p. 14 top right
Willow Creek: p. 15 top
The Foursquare Church: p. 19
Mary Evans Picture Library: p. 23
World Council of Churches: p. 28

**All other maps and illustrations:**
Tim Dowley Associates

# Contents

# Introduction

As social historians attempt to make sense of the last century, views will be many, and revisionist historiographers will put interpretive capstones on their efforts by suggesting that the issues are too complex for reductionistic approaches. However, one thing is unmistakable: the twentieth century witnessed the collapse of the noble experiment that was inaugurated in the Renaissance and that flowered in the eighteenth century. The Enlightenment was rooted in the assumption that the blightedness of the human soul, a long-held assumption in Christendom, was a categorical mistake. Enlightenment philosophy held that if humankind could be loosed from the shackles of external authorities and tradition, becoming free to plumb the labyrinth of what was within, then the ravages of the beastly nature could be ameliorated and a world of inevitable progress in sobriety and peace would be at our doorstep. The "saviors" of humankind would be character training—the university, science, and technology.

**Successes of Enlightenment**

The enormous successes that the Enlightenment brought about in the modern era have been impressive. Who does not marvel at the wonders of modern medicine, space stations, and computer technology? However, the success of Enlightenment thinking was its ultimate unraveling. While improving the social environment of humankind in the West, Enlightenment assumptions emptied the soul. Imagination was eclipsed by reason; there was, resultantly, no place for mystery and faith, only molecules. In the arid wasteland of mathematics and logic, religious attempts to hang on to religious expression by emptying it of its historic content, and reducing it to mere morals, do-good-to-others stuff, share the colossal blame due the Enlightenment. The result is that the modern world has gone insane. The beast within has not been tamed; in fact, it could be argued that advances in the sciences, particularly in the military arena, have not civilized humankind's more beastly aspects, such as greed, desire for control, and hate. G. K. Chesterton said poetically, "What does breed insanity is reason. . . . The general fact is simple. Poetry is sane because it floats easily in an infinite sea, reason seeks to cross the infinite sea, and so make it finite" (*Orthodoxy* [Whitefish, MT: Kessinger Publishing, 2004], 8).

**Christian failure**

One great benefit of the collapse of the adoration of the mental processes, whether in the sciences or religion, is the opening of the possibility of transcendence, mystery, something that captures imagination and opens an immateriality that inspires. The failure of the Christian reaction to the Enlightenment has been that Christians have seen faith through the lens of arguments and proofs rather than regarding it as something ultimately beyond human grasp. Other reactions have been to empty that belief of its historic content by reducing the focus of the Christian faith to the correction of cultural deficiencies, or to stress the emotive aspects of true faith to the detriment of the cognitive or social implications.

The collapse of the Enlightenment in the twentieth century has the potential of returning the world to sanity, though this is only one of the possible options. However one seeks to express social prophecy, Christianity cannot afford to be delineated in confident rational categories alone.

# The Trauma of War

The essence of the Enlightenment was its postulation that human potential could be unlimited; science and technology became the "new gospel," self-reliance the new creed. Coupled with this optimistic analysis was the notion of progress. Whether it was Hegel's "*Geist*" or Darwin's theory of favorable mutations applied to the social sciences, improvement in society as a whole, and individuals within it, was within our grasp. All that was lacking was time. The fatal flaw, among lesser ones, was the relativity of change. Nothing could be static or permanent any longer.

The issue of the inevitability of human progress had its death knell sounded with social and global engineering. The wars of the nineteenth century paled in comparison to the wars, holocausts, and ethnic cleansings of the twentieth century. Faith in human progress was divorced from the brutality of modern weapons and the bestiality of the human heart.

**A scene of destruction and desolation on the Western Front in France during World War I.**

## Art and disillusion

It was not the global chaos that signaled disillusion, it was art. From Impressionism, Ash Can art, and Cubism; the twelve tonal music of jazz; new dance crazes such as the Charleston, the "Bear," the "Fox," and the "Bunny"; changing hemlines and the absence of waistlines in fashion, experimentation and improvisation spelled the decline of tradition and convention.

The changes that artists depicted concerning the nature of reality and the locus of truth, though occurring in the early twentieth century, did not surface as fully developed behavioral patterns in the United States until the 1950s and 1960s. The two great wars of the century and the devastating Depression between them delayed cultural change at the popular level. Then, the enormous prosperity, fueled by unimaginable technological advances, created a world that the Enlightenment had promised. But what was sacrificed along the way was cultural cohesiveness and corporate identity. The Enlightenment brought untold wealth, travel opportunity, and gadgets, but the cost was social stability and community.

**The Surrealist painter Salvador Dali (1904–1989) at work in his studio.**

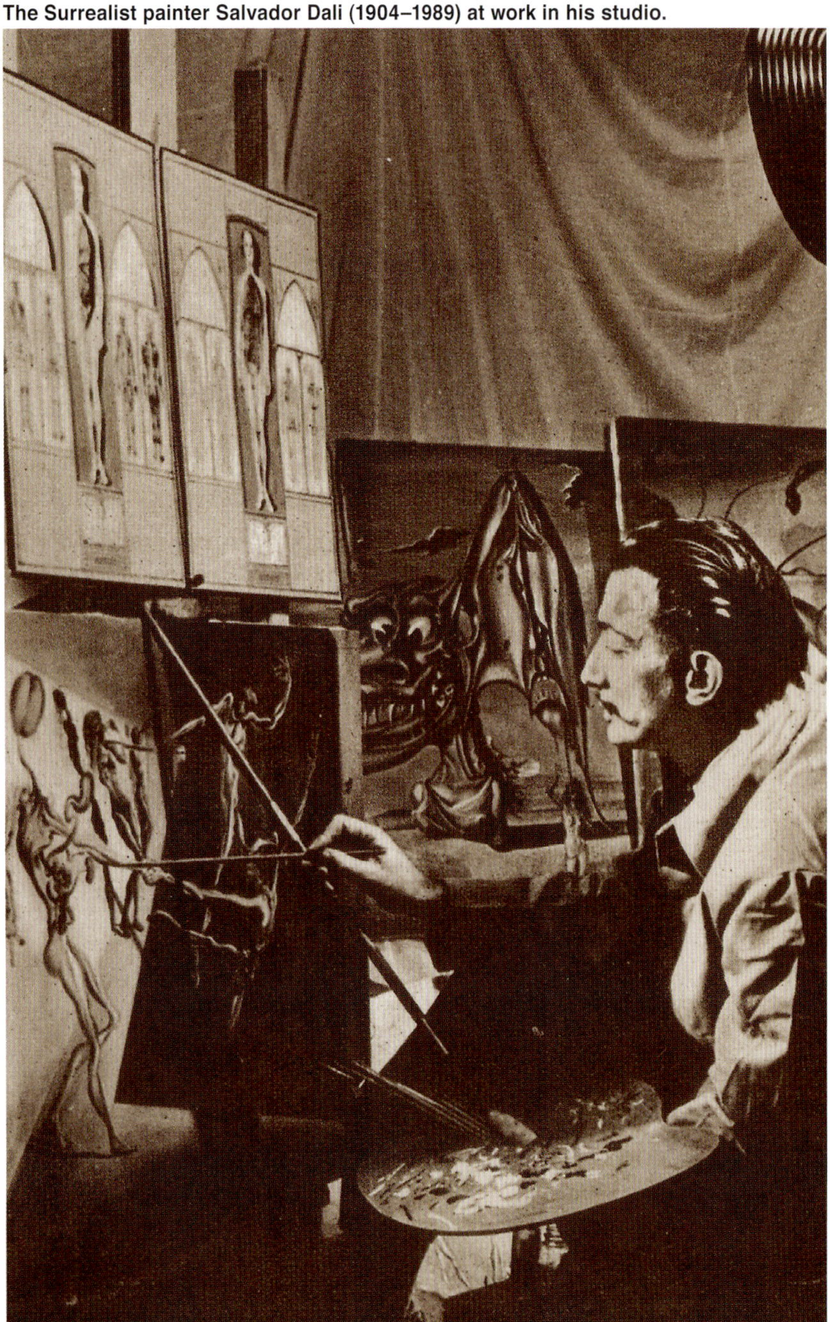

## Decline of religion

In retrospect, it is now clear that the Enlightenment was an enormous challenge to the time-honored place of religion as the interpreter of the transcendence that explained the exigencies of life and provided hope in the midst of despair. Attempts to maintain the centrality of religion (Orthodox, Protestant, or Roman Catholic) in everyday life has failed. The story of the loss of religion as the determinant of values and hope is the task before us. Despite struggling to prevent the inroads of the Enlightenment, modifying the faith so as not to be discredited by it, or resisting change in spite of mounting evidence to the contrary, the result was the same. Whether it is the concessive adaptation of religion or valiant resistance to change, religion has been reduced to one among many competitive ideas in a free market smorgasbord. The so-called third place, the place to gather other than home and work is no longer the church; it increasingly is, for example, the new safe place for relationship building—a "community" without personal attachments or social commitment: the online community.

# Karl Barth (1886–1968)

Arguably Karl Barth was the most influential theologian of the twentieth century. Swiss born and trained in Bern, Berlin, and Marburg under outstanding religious scholars of his day, he became disillusioned with his liberal training as he sought to pastor flocks in Geneva and Safenwil in the context of the horrors of World War I. In 1919 he published *Der Romerbrief* (*The Letter to the Romans*), a manifesto for a return to a transcendent God, the God of Holy Scripture, revealed in the Christ event. He would eventually come to describe nineteenth-century German theology as "a monologue of the soul with its own divinity." He explained the impact of his small book, a second edition published in 1922, as that like a man climbing a dark tower who reached out to steady himself only to eventually realize that he had grasped a rope for support and awakened the whole countryside with the sound of a great bell.

**Barth and Hitler**

This publication catapulted Barth from the pastorate to the university where he held posts both at Munster and Bonn. His refusal to give loyalty to Adolf Hitler and his participation in the *Barmen Declaration* (1934) led to his dismissal from Bonn in 1935. He was subsequently called to the chair of theology in Basel, Switzerland, where he served until his retirement in 1961.

Barth's unfinished magnum opus was *The Church Dogmatics*, a massive literary interaction with the history of Christian thought, with Catholic and Protestant thinkers as well as secular scholars. The work reflects the author's own religious pilgrimage; he seemed to discover and understand as he wrote. Therefore, the work is not homogeneous; it is a record of his developing, changing understanding. He strove to be biblical and thought that he was so. No other theologian in the twentieth century quoted more Scripture or included more

**Barth's refusal to give loyalty to Hitler led to his dismissal from Bonn in 1935.**

**Karl Barth (1886–1968).**

exegetical material in his theology than Barth.

**Barth vs. Schleiermacher**

The thrust of his polemics was against Friedrich Schleiermacher (1768–1834), the fountainhead of nineteenth-century German theology. Barth said of him that he did not found a school, but an era. He felt that it was Schleiermacher's attempt to establish the tenets of religion in subjectivism that set a trend, though modified by the Ritschlians who sought a more factual basis for religion, that led to religion's demise. (Materialists like Strauss and Marx rejected the whole enterprise as a mental disorder.) For Barth, religion must begin in the self-disclosure of God. True religion must begin in faith, seeking understanding with a humble heart, not with a finite quest for the infinite.

In comparison to the trend of theology in the hands of the Ritschlians, or the History of Religions approach, which reduced theology to ethics and God to a mirror-reflection of its creators, Barth assumed the utter transcendence of God as the first truth of true religion. To the Reformed theologian in Barth, God is wholly other. He is incomprehensible and can only be known within the limitations of His own self-disclosure. God has revealed Himself in the person of Jesus Christ, the true God and true Man; this is the central truth of true religion. Though not to be identified with the revelation of God, the Bible is the witness of God in Christ, the Word of God. The revelation of God is beyond the Bible, yet never in contradistinction to it.

**German Protestant theologian Friedrich Schleiermacher (1768–1834) as a young man.**

**Savior of orthodoxy?**

In many ways, Barth was both a critic of and an improvement over many of his predecessors. However, he has been received with mixed reviews from his contemporaries. Some have hailed him as the "savior" of an orthodoxy caught in the web of rationalism and natural theology; others have said that he offered little improvement over those he invested so much energy confronting.

It was not so much Barth's particular understanding of Christianity that influenced a century of theologians, as it was his methodological approach. According to Barth, the Bible is not the Word of God until Christ, who alone is the Word of God, is revealed through it in the conjunction of the finite and fallible with the infinite and infallible. The issue of the integrity of Scripture as a whole did not concern him. In Barth's view, the Bible is the words of men; the words of men can become the Word of God. The weakness of Barth's approach to religious truth is that it appears to open the door to subjectivism and shut the door to absolute, objective religious truth. For the Bible to witness to Christ requires a personal, individual crisis experience. Since no two revelations of Christ through the witness to the Word need be the same, religious content becomes relative and the message about Christ not one, but many. Whatever may be said of Barth's conclusions, two things are evident: first, he successfully confronted nineteenth-century liberalism and, in doing so, altered its direction, though he was not able to demolish it; and, second, his theology is profoundly Christocentric and conservative in that regard.

# The Faces of Barthianism

It was an indictment of Barth's method of verification that when asked on one occasion if he was a Barthian, he denied it. That is, during his visit to the United States in the early 1960s, when he was unwilling to identify with many of his students' conclusions, Barth seems to have unleashed a sense that the Bible could enshrine an authentic revelation from God; but the application of his method led to conflicting conclusions as to what that revelation might be.

In the thought of Emil Brunner (1889–1966), the Swiss theologian and pastor in Zurich, revelation was not to be limited to an encounter between God's revelation in his Son, man the sinner, and the Bible in the Christ event; religious knowledge was also deposited in natural revelation. The thought of a Christ-revelation outside the Bible was abhorrent to Barth, who was adamant that revelation is only in Christ. Brunner was unwilling to accept the notion of a radical disjunction between grace and human consciousness. At the moment of crisis, the Bible became the Word of God to Barth. Though the Bible was revelation, it was not to be viewed as infallible, even in the Christ event.

Dietrich Bonhoeffer (1906–1945).

### Barth vs. Bultmann

Barth's most sustained criticism of a contemporary was reserved for Rudolph Bultmann (1884–1976). He was, in many ways, a kind of collage of ideas from the nineteenth-century scholars that Barth resisted. Trained in the great German universities of Tubingen, Berlin, and Marburg, his teaching spanned several decades, though he ended his career at Marburg (1921–1951). Rejecting Barth's notion that the infallible Word was transfigured into the Word of God in Christ, Bultmann sought to find behind the text of the Bible its original message. The Bible was never more than a text with a distorted heritage and layers of mythology that had obscured a simple story. Behind the Bible was a message, a kerygma, which could be known if the accretions could be eliminated. The means of recognizing the message behind the Bible is a radically subjective assessment akin to Schleiermacher's approach and as denigrating to the Bible as David Strauss's view.

It is little wonder, with such trends in the universities, that Bultmann's later years were characterized by despair over the weakened state of the German churches.

A more conservative expression of Barth's influence is evident in Thomas F. Torrance (1913–2007), professor of Christian theology at the University of Edinburgh. At the popular level, Dietrich Bonhoeffer (1906–1945), the much-celebrated martyr to Nazi tyranny, continues to influence Christendom through his writings, particularly *The Cost of Discipleship* and *Letters and Papers from Prison*. The former has become a modern classic on what it means to follow Christ, decrying the notion of "cheap grace" as opposed to "costly grace."

# The Fortunes of American Protestantism

In retrospect, the modern era from a religious perspective has been very much about how to maintain the time-honored place and relevance of the Christian faith in a world that changed with the rise of science and philosophy (natural revelation). If there is a place for religion that denigrates the thought of human independence, the need of a redeemer other than technology, what must the new face of that faith look like?

From the perspective of western cultural values, Christianity in whatever form it may disguise itself has failed. The respect and appreciation for the Bible, characteristic of the medieval and Reformation eras, whether Protestant or Roman Catholic, is past. The divisions within Christianity in the twentieth century now appear to have been intramural squabbles. All parties lost the very thing they sought to sustain in combating each other, an exalted place for religion in postmodern social values.

**American Protestant Liberalism**

The American liberal movement, the New Theology, was an attempt by progressive churchmen to preserve the faith by meeting the challenges of modernism with change. Unfortunately, the cost of sustaining the popularity of religion was the paring away of traditional theological content. The movement has gone through three discernible epochs in North America: the era of emergence (1880–1930), the era of triumph (1930–1960), and the era of disintegration (1960–present).

In a world of rapid new discoveries and inventions, traditional interpretations of the Bible appeared so embarrassing that Christianity was threatened, at least in the view of some. The solution was to adopt a view of the Bible articulated by the German Ritschlian scholars, a Bible within the Bible. Objectionable parts (such as a six-day creation, a Noahic flood, the imprecatory Psalms, the great whale story of Jonah, the seeming sanction of slavery and polygamy) could simply be labeled as error. The "tail" that wagged the theological "dog" was science, which was confused with common sense.

Wall painting from Turkey of Jonah being swallowed by the great fish. Liberal scholars labeled such Bible stories as "error."

Jesus was still central in the new faith, but He was seen as the flower of humanity and not as God in the flesh. He became a wonderful example of moral virtue and self-sacrifice. The content of the Bible, consistent with that picture of Him, was the "real Bible" and the rest was myth. Shailer Mathews (1863–1941), professor at the University of Chicago, defined the movement as an "undertaking to adjust Christianity to modern needs by changing the emphasis in its message" (*Faith of a Modernist* [1925], 22).

The liberal movement in Protestant theology gained access to important teaching positions in the northern denominational seminaries (e.g., Baptist, Methodist, Presbyterian) in the early decades of the twentieth century as well as prominent posts in denominational hierarchies. By the 1920s the new emphases were evident in the churches. Differences led to conflict and conflict to the triumph of liberalism. The clash of divergent factions within the great denominations ended as the Great Depression strangled the nation. For many traditionalists, the losses had eschatological portent; surely the end of all things was near. One thing was as blatant as H. L. Mencken's ridicule of conservatives as anti-intellectual country bumpkins: traditional concepts of religious value were gone, perhaps forever, from mainstream America.

**Reinhold Niebuhr found the Puritan Jonathan Edwards (1703–1758) insightful.**

**Paul Tillich (1886–1965).**

### Beyond liberalism

In the era of the triumph of liberalism on the North American scene, in the decades following the First World War, voices emerged arguing that liberalism needed a mid-course change. The components of inevitable progress and human improvability seemed shattered by the Great War. In one of the most important sermons of the era, "The Church Must Go Beyond Liberalism" (1935), Harry Emerson Fosdick (1878–1969), a prominent New York pastor and national radio voice, called for a "new liberalism" that would challenge the prevailing secular culture.

The refacing of liberalism, dubbed "neo-liberalism," would dominate theology from the 1930s to the 1960s. Borrowing interpretative insights from the broad neo-orthodox movement, neo-liberal scholars rejected the overemphasis in the nineteenth century on the immanence of God, an overly optimistic view of human nature, and the notion of inevitable progress. Some, such as Reinhold Niebuhr (1892–1971), pastor and seminary professor, found the Puritan Jonathan Edwards insightful. For Niebuhr, the social problems of the day could not be solved by the rigorous application of reason alone; it required political solutions. Crafted by Walter Marshall Horton (1895–1965) of Oberlin College, John C. Bennett (1902–1994), and H. P. Van Dusen (1897–1975) of Union Seminary, New York, a theology emerged for the churches devoid of the bubbly optimism of old liberal rhetoric, as well as the harsh criticism of conservatives as a group of psychological misfits who cling to a forever-gone past because they fear change.

Sometimes called "Realistic Theology" because it seemed to take the Bible more seriously and spoke of it more respectfully, it remained very much characterized by old assumptions in a new dress. Jesus Christ was more like God than humankind, but He remained outside the pale of true deity. Advocates rejected the notion of a salvation through science, but sin remained moral selfishness and salvation societal harmony.

In the radical 1960s, the decade of enormous societal unrest, liberalism began to fracture as a movement. It no longer possessed a cohesive set of values and it disintegrated into competing factions and fad theologies. The more radical insights of Bultmann seemed to influence theologians in the movement more than the conserving influence of Barth.

Various forms of liberation or empowerment theologies emerged such as Black Theology, Feminist Theology, God-Is-Dead Theology, and Theology of the Poor. Each used the Bible, but did so in a manner that saw within it their own message and neglected other vast portions. The theological method adopted in these theologies, though rarely in their conclusions, was Rudolph Bultmann's.

Among other expressions of the fracturing liberal movement were a rash of short-lived, momentarily popular attempts to separate the essential message of the Bible from the Bible. Examples of these were Teilhard de Chardin's Theology of Evolution and Wilhelm Moltmann's Theology of Hope. What was seemingly always missing was the centrality of the incarnate Christ, the utter hopelessness of a sinful race, the great propitiatory event of Calvary, and hope of a heaven beyond the exigencies of this life. What the Bible set forth as its essential message they missed; what they emphasized missed the major point. In effect, in the recent liberal tradition there are many "Bibles."

Two popular examples of the disintegration of liberalism, though they have now lost their mystique, is Paul Tillich's Theology of Being in the 1960s and Process Theology in the 1980s and 1990s. Tillich's (1886–1965) conclusions were reminiscent of Ludwig Feuerbach of the previous century. Theology was reduced to psychological symbolism. God is not real; he is a symbol of human ultimate concerns and needs, as is the human invention of the Trinity. Jesus Christ is only a God-intoxicated man, a psychologically whole person.

Process Theology reflected the huge shift in epistemology as the modern era faded into postmodernism. Unlike theologies before it, rooted in Newtonian science, Process Theology is rooted in Heisenberg, Planck, and Einstein's world of indeterminacy, relativity, and Quantum physics.

Applied to religion, there is indeterminacy in God. God is gaining understanding as the future evolves into the present. This understanding of God, it is argued, is more comforting to people because God truly identifies with human weaknesses and ignorance.

### American Protestant Evangelicalism

Liberalism is a movement that has lost its way. It lacks a uniform core of affirmations, a concise goal, and a clear means for obtaining it.

Evangelicalism shares much the same experience as its counterpart, American liberalism. The two are deeply intertwined seeking the same end, the preservation of a vital form of Christian faith. Both have recently shown evidence of stumbling. The history of evangelicalism can be divided into four periods: a period of emergence (1880–1910), a period of conflict (1910–1930), a period of resurgence (1930–1980), and a period of fracturing (1980–present). In retrospect, it is now evident that the movement was rooted in nineteenth-century revivalism and the Common Sense tradition, catapulted into existence by its resistance to liberalism, and expressed in transdenominational alliances and paraecclesiastical mission organizations.

Tensions within American denominational Christianity began to surface in the 1880s. New England Congregationalists seem to have been the first to struggle over appropriate accommodation to the rise of the sciences and the general mood of buoyant optimism and self-sufficiency that gripped the nation, most particularly their effect upon the way the Bible should be understood. Fractures could be detected in the foundation stones of the Presbyterian and Methodist churches as well.

**J. Gresham Machen (1881–1937), staunch opponent of theological liberalism.**

**Charles Fuller breaks the turf in preparation for building Fuller Theological Seminary, Los Angeles, California.**

### Denominations divide

In the post–world war era of the twenties, the denominational fissures became a chasm of open conflict. In essence what was at stake was the direction of the great, large denominational bodies. Liberals were convinced that theological change and cultural accommodation would keep Christianity a viable, relevant force in the nation. Conservatives, sometimes called fundamentalists or evangelicals (the terms being synonymous at this early stage), were horrified at the implication of Christianity devoid of historic orthodox doctrine. In the mind of J. Gresham Machen (1881–1937), the Presbyterian scholar, whatever

Carl F. H. Henry (1913–2003), evangelical intellectual statesman.

The American evangelist Billy Graham (b. 1918), most prominent figure among the second generation of evangelical leaders of the mid twentieth century.

one would call the liberal tradition, it should not be thought of as Christian. As the nation tumbled under the shock of the stock market crash of 1929 and struggled with the implications of the Great Depression, one thing became clear: the liberal element in the northern mainline bodies had gained control of the denominational hierarchies, publication societies, mission boards, and educational centers. The situation was as bleak as the plight of the farmer in the Great Dust Bowl who left all for the orange groves of southern California and a new life.

The evangelical/fundamentalist/conservative element faced another crisis. Having lost the struggle with liberalism denominationally, what were they to do? Though many stayed within the mainline churches to participate as laity or serve as leaders, others felt the need for more strictly conservative churches. The result was that in the 1930s and 1940s, many small denominational splinter groups were established (Baptist, Presbyterian, Methodist, et al.), as well as were a host of independent churches, often called community, Bible, or fellowship churches. With them came new publication societies, mission boards, and educational institutions.

### New groupings

Though many new groups formed at this time, they were quite small. This presented a problem in outreach; further, the liberal movement had a collective organization, the Federal Council of Churches (now National Council of Churches), which claimed to be the voice of Christianity in America. Recognizing the need for cooperative unity several umbrella agencies were formed. The most prolific of these was the National Association of Evangelicals (1942). Evangelicals began to experience a renaissance of fortunes in America, though the collective expression of its vitality was often not in the churches, but in the proliferation of paraecclesiastical agencies, whether educational institutions or evangelistic organizations.

As the 1930s faded into the 40s and 50s, a second generation of leaders emerged that envisioned an even brighter day. The dream was to put a new, positive face on the movement that would challenge the liberal movement's hegemony and give the nation both a biblically accurate and culturally concerned Christianity. The intellectual statesman behind it was Carl F. H. Henry (1913–2003), whose *Uneasy Conscience of a Modern Fundamentalism* (1947) was the movement's catalyst. Billy Graham (b. 1918) was the most prominent public figure, *Christianity Today* (1956) the literary voice, and Fuller Theological Seminary (1947) its educational citadel. The glue of the movement resided in a simple creed that affirmed the basic conservative affirmations of historic Christianity while minimizing the importance of denominational distinctives and the community of the fellowship of individual churches. It was the triumph of the nineteenth-century revivalist spirit and the paraecclesiastical enterprise.

The rhetoric of the movement was frequently as critical as it was naively optimistic. As a result of the positions its advocates affirmed, it caused division in the ranks. What was argued was that the conservative, fundamentalist, evangelical movement had been a loose coalition whose unity resided in a mutual hostility to liberalism. The triumph of liberalism, as well as the reciprocal criticisms of the demeanor and policies of some in the coalition, destroyed it. Terms once viewed as synonymous, fundamentalist and evangelical became parties that were mutually hostile, and philosophically and culturally divergent.

**Dr. J. I. Packer (b. 1926), reformed theologian and evangelical writer.**

**Bill Bright (1921–2003), founder of the student evangelistic organization Campus Crusade.**

**Evangelicalism resurgent**

*Time* magazine recognized the resurgence of evangelicalism, announcing 1976 as the "Year of the Evangelical." However, the movement had already begun to fracture with an in-house controversy over the integrity of the Bible and the creation of the Council on Biblical Inerrancy. In some ways evangelicalism found itself where American

Bill Hybels (b. 1951), pastor of Willow Creek Community Church, Chicago, Illinois, one of the largest megachurches in the USA.

Christianity was in the 1890s—divided over how the Bible was to be read, pillaged by the issues of Feminist Theology, and polarized over doubts about traditional conceptions of the doctrine of God and theism. The term evangelicalism lost, if it ever possessed it, a recognizable identity.

Since the theory of an evangelical unity through an emphasis on a few important essentials seems to have failed, the "movement" has devolved into a labyrinth of competing theories of sacred renewalism. Some see little hope for Christianity's renaissance without a "new reformation." In this view, the church's primary problem is that it has imbibed the mores and values of the culture while losing it historic orthodox message.

**The way ahead?**

Others believe that the hope of rebirth is in cultural accommodation and a "seeker friendly" philosophy of ministry that remains Christian, but is not "limited" by traditional styles of worship and symbolism. For some, the allegorical "Rosetta Stone" is to return to primitive patterns of doing church evident in the second and third centuries. A reaction to the megachurch movement, the Emergent Church movement seeks to return to church smallness, discipleship and discipline, and community consciousness. For others the quest for rootedness has led them to the Protestant liturgical churches (i.e., Episcopalian, Lutheran, Presbyterian). Others have entered the Roman Catholic and Orthodox communities. Cultural Christianity, in this case the noisy, often shallow individualism of the American spirit (i.e., evangelicalism) has become a bit too much for many.

Another solution, a rather novel one to say the least, is to return to the Christian world before the emergence of the paraecclesiastical model of ministry. That means placing the locus of Christian identity in the local church or denomination where a more holistic expression of biblical understanding and a particular heritage can be extolled. The way to effect cultural change, according to this theory, is not a grand series of meetings, an emphasis of cultlike personalities, or cultural compromise. With doctrinal integrity to combat theological reductionism, with emphasis on the pastoral role, and with the dynamic of the community of the saints coupled with societal awareness and concern, renewal of the church—if not of the whole of society—may come.

Dr. Billy Graham preaches to a crowd of 1,100,000 people at Yoido Plaza, Seoul, Korea.

GREENLAND
CANADA
USA
ICELAND
SWEDEN
NORWAY
UNITED KINGDOM
DENMARK
AUSTRIA
NETHERLANDS
IRELAND
BELGIUM
LUXEMBOURG
GERMANY
FRANCE
SWITZERLAND
SLOVENIA
PORTUGAL
SPAIN
ANDORRA
ITALY
ATLANTIC OCEAN
TUNISIA
MOROCCO
LIBY
ALGERIA
WESTERN SAHARA
MAURETANIA
MALI
NIGE
SENEGAL
GAMBIA
BURKINA FASO
GUINEA-BISSAU
GUINEA
NIGERIA
SIERRA LEONE
IVORY COAST
GHANA
TOGO
BENIN
LIBERIA
CAMEROON
EQUATORIAL GUINEA
GABON
ANGOLA
NAMIBIA
MEXICO
CUBA
DOMINICAN REPUBLIC
JAMAICA
PUERTO RICO
HAITI
BELIZE
HONDURAS
GUATEMALA
NICARAGUA
EL SALVADOR
COSTA RICA
PANAMA
TRINIDAD & TOBAGO
VENEZUELA
GUYANA
SURINAM
FRENCH GUIANA
COLOMBIA
ECUADOR
PACIFIC OCEAN
BRAZIL
PERU
BOLIVIA
CHILE
PARAGUAY
ARGENTINA
URUGUAY
Percentage annual church growth, c.1990
Very rapid (over 5%)
Rapid (3–5%)
Moderate (1–3%)
Little or nil (0–1%)
Decline (less than 0%)
0 2000 4000 km
0 800 1600 2400 miles

# Christianity Worldwide

around the turn of the twenty-first century

# American Protestant Mainline Denominationalism

In recent decades the mainline churches have experienced the growing cultural disinterest in Christianity (arguably the result of the loss of doctrinal integrity). The more liberal the denominational policies of a group, the greater the numerical decline. For example, the American Baptist Church, USA (northern Baptists), between 1990 and 2003 had a drop in membership of over 106,000 (6.8%); the Episcopal Church lost over 12,000 (4.9%); and the United Methodist Church lost over 757,000 (8.3%). Some denominations recorded double-digit decline: the Disciples of Christ (189,000 or 26.7%); the Presbyterian Church, USA (435,000 or 14.8%); and the United Church of Christ (285,000 or 17%).

What is somewhat ironic is that denominational decline has occurred on not a few occasions in spite of major ecclesiastical mergers that brought together larger groups under a single title. In 1968, the United Methodist Church came into existence in the merger of the Methodist Church and the Evangelical United Brethren. The Congregational Church of New England experienced two mergers in the last century, the latest (1957) with the Evangelical and Reformed Church to become the United Church of Christ. In 1982 the Northern and Southern Presbyterian communities merged to become the Presbyterian Church USA.

**President George W. Bush meets Southern Baptist leaders in the White House, Washington, D.C.**

### Denominations in turmoil

Since World War II three denominational bodies have experienced turmoil over theology. Beginning in the 1940s, the Presbyterian Church South (the PCUS) began a struggle that ended in schism in 1972. A conservative splinter group was formed, the Presbyterian Church in America, and the southern and northern bodies merged in 1982 to form the PCUSA.

In the 1960s and 1970s, theological turmoil gripped the Lutheran Church, Missouri Synod, focused on discontent at Concordia Theological Seminary, St. Louis. After years of difficulties and the founding of the more latitudinal Seminix (1974), Seminary in Exile, the denomination experienced schism with the establishment of the Association of Evangelical Lutheran Churches (AELC) in 1976. In 1988 three progressive Lutheran bodies—the AELC, the American Lutheran Church, and the Lutheran Church in America—merged to become the Evangelical Lutheran Churches of America.

### The Southern Baptists

Controversy troubled the Southern Baptist Convention, the largest Protestant denomination in America, in the 1970s and 1980s. Fearing a progressive takeover, conservatives (fundamentalists) waged a political struggle to regain control of the denomination's boards. At the convention level, as well as within the seminaries, conservatives have been successful in reestablishing hegemony; at the state level they have not. Signs of progressive discouragement with the direction of the convention have been the withholding of money from denominational causes (thus limiting their voting power at the convention level), the creation of a rival educational institution, and the threat of creating a new denomination. The SBC is one of the very rare examples in history where liberal threats have been throttled and conservatism sustained.

# The Charismatic Movements

With roots in eighteenth-century Methodism, as well as the nineteenth-century American revivalist tradition, the Charismatic Movement has become a rapidly growing, exceedingly diverse, global phenomenon. The fertile soil out of which it sprang was the quest for a deeper experience of Christ and empowerment for service. Some within American Methodism felt a spiritual dullness creeping over the church and identified the cause as a lack of a second, subsequent reinvigorating experience of divine grace. As taught by Phoebe Palmer (1807–1874), every Christian needed two crises experiences with God, one to redeem and one to cleanse. Hannah Pearsall Smith (1832–1911) spoke of the "secret" to spiritual vitality; William E. Boardman (1810–1866), a Presbyterian, of a "higher Christian life." It was achieved through an ever-present self-dedication to God.

**Holiness movements**

These emphases coalesced within American Methodism as the National Holiness Movement (1867). Often critical of the state of the church and possessing a separatist, even judgmental, spirit, the holiness faction clashed with the entrenched hierarchy of the church. Gradually, holiness advocates separated from Methodism and formed splinter holiness denominations, such as the Church of the Nazarene (1895), Pilgrim Holiness Church (a merger of the Holiness Christian Church [1882] and the International Holiness Union [1897] in 1919), the Pentecostal Holiness Church (1900), and the Holiness Church (1892).

Within the holiness movement, some had come to experience what was an additional work of grace that would eventually be identified with the apostles' experience in Acts 2 with the evidence of speech in an unknown language. The movement was early denominated as the Latter Rain Revival and the Apostolic Faith Movement. It was called the Latter Rain Revival because its advocates believed that they were near the end of human history before the Lord's return that would be immediately preceded by a global revival. It was denominated the Apostolic Faith Movement because of the belief that empowerment for the global revival would come through the reemergence of first-century miraculous signs and wonders.

**Pentecostal precursors**

While precursors of the movement can be identified through the centuries, the beginning of the twentieth-century phenomena is generally identified with the work of Charles Fox Parham (1873–1929) of the Bethel Bible Institute (1901), Topeka, Kansas, and the Azusa Revivals (1906–1909) in Los Angeles, California. Parham connected the Acts 2 experience with a spiritual endowment for service, a third work of grace with

Aimee Semple McPherson (1890–1944), the founder of the Four Square Gospel Church (1923).

"signs following." The first to speak of tongues as evidence of a post-conversion Spirit baptism was Agnes Ozman (1870–1937) of the Fire Baptized Holiness Church. The new teaching spread through the holiness churches, most demonstrably under William J. Seymour (1870–1922), a follower of Parham, who spearheaded the international explosion of the movement in Los Angeles. Many came with a spiritual emptiness to his meetings to leave renewed.

### Assemblies of God

A major step in the development of the movement that sought to bring unity and ministerial standardization was the creation of the Assemblies of God (1914). Many early Pentecostals came from a Methodist-holiness background which saw the Pentecostal experience as a third work of grace. However, Pentecostals were not monolithic in many of their beliefs concerning the meaning and sequence of the needed empowerment. Some early Pentecostals from a Christian and Missionary Alliance embraced the concept that salvation and sanctification occurred in one act of faith and so they anticipated a second work only. This was called the "finished work." This controversy created a twofold polarization in the movement. The Assemblies did much to bring uniformity, standardization, and protection from radical excesses.

A second division came to the burgeoning movement in 1916, causing the Assemblies to adopt a doctrinal statement as new teaching proved exceedingly disruptive in the churches. Called the Unitarian or "Jesus Only" Pentecostalism, advocates embraced a view that has affinities to ancient modalism. It seemed to reject the Trinity and argued that Jesus alone is God and that baptism should be only in Jesus' name. The largest of this expression of classical Pentecostalism is the United Pentecostal Church (1945).

### Hostilities lessen

With the passing of decades, the initial hostilities between Pentecostals and non-Pentecostals lessened as the movement matured and as the liberal movement in American theology threatened to engulf them both. A major breakthrough came when several Pentecostal bodies, principally the Assemblies of God, joined the National Association of Evangelicals (1943). Today the largest Pentecostal denomination is the Church of God in Christ (1910), a schism from a holiness group, founded by Charles H. Mason (1865–1949). The second largest is the Assemblies of God. The most prominent evangelist of the era of early Pentecostalism,

much in the tradition of Mary Wordsworth-Etter (1844–1924), was Aimee Semple McPherson (1890–1944), the founder of the Four Square Gospel Church (1923).

The fervent expectation of the soon return of Christ that fueled the movement began to wane in the 1940s; a generation was passing away and the plethora of miracles had faded into a trickle. Pentecostals longed for a reawakening. The transition to a new era, sometimes called the Second Wave, was the healing tent revival movement made popular by Oral Roberts (1918–2009), Charles Branham (1909–1965), Gordon Lindsay (1906–1973), Asa A. Allen (1911–1970), and a host of others. Out of this movement, which disintegrated in the 1950s, came the Full Gospel Businessmen's Fellowship founded by Oral Roberts and Demos Shakarian (1913–1993). It sought to regulate the healing movement, but in retrospect became the impetus for a new trend. An example of the shift can be seen in the ministry of Roberts, who changed the name of his organization from Healing Wings to the Oral Roberts Evangelistic Association, transitioned from tents to hotel ballrooms, joined the United Methodist Church,

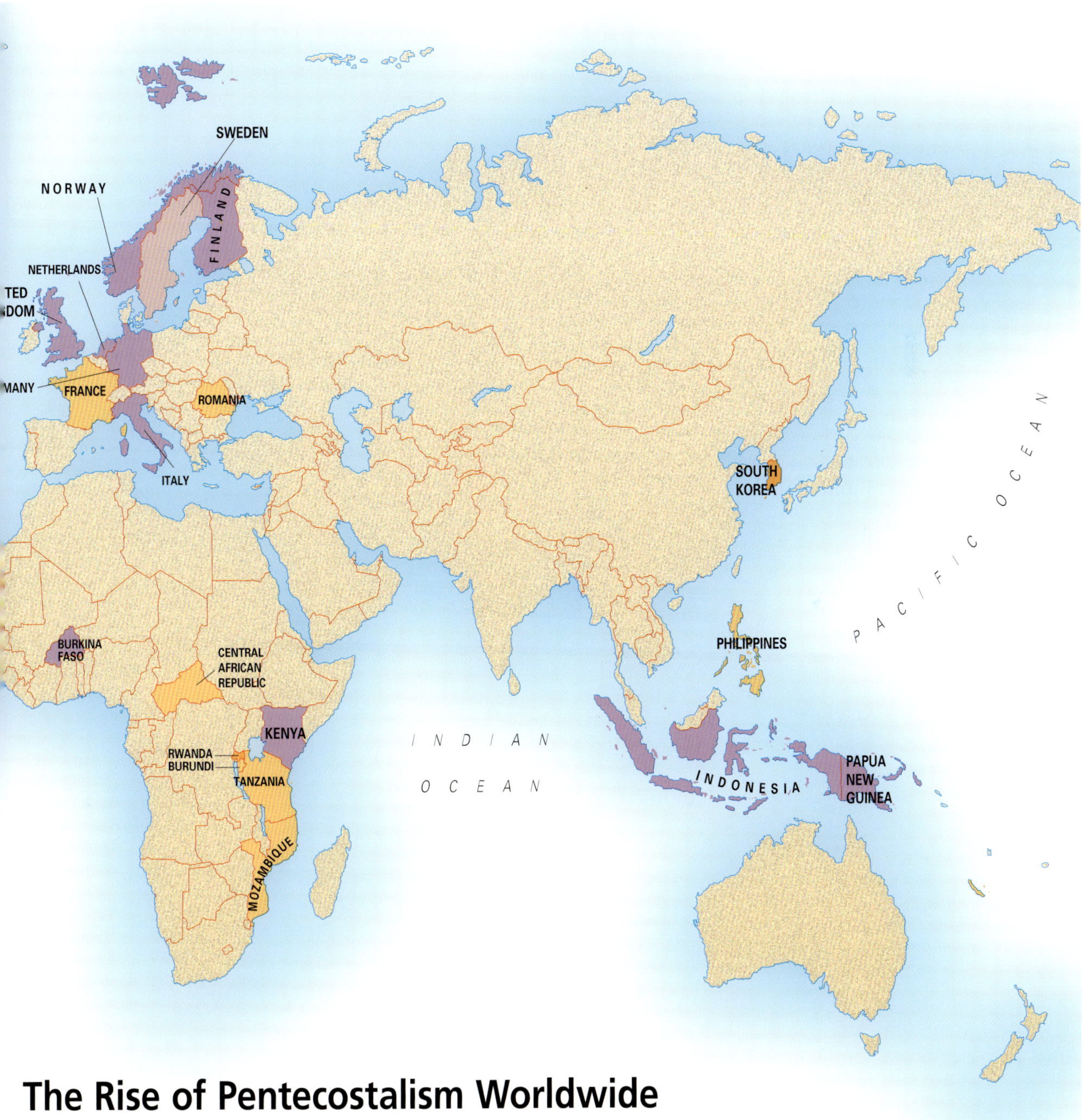


# The Rise of Pentecostalism Worldwide

and founded a university. Parts of classical Pentecostalism were being reinvigorated in what has been called the Charismatic Movement. Perhaps a better title would be the Renewalist Movement of the 1960s and 1970s.

### The Second Wave

The Renewalist, or Second Wave, Movement was the penetration of the spirituality of the Pentecost-experience into the traditional, and declining, mainline churches. Not only was the new expression of the charismatic phenomena within the mainline; it was less insistent on doctrinal rigidity and less noisy than its predecessor. Speaking in tongues was not required to certify the experience of newfound joy and power, and the locus shifted away from large meetings to small Bible study groups with a facilitator.

Beginning in the late 1960s, in the rectorship of Dennis Bennett (1917–1991), a California Episcopalian cleric, the movement seemed to breathe new vitality into almost all branches of mainline Protestantism in America and around the world. A galaxy of new names became identified with this new phase of the larger movement though, unlike the previous one, it was much more decentralized. Kathryn Kuhlman (1907–1976) was, perhaps, the most prominent voice in the realm of healing ministry, but others were David Du Plessis (1905–1987), called "Mr. International Pentecost"; Michael Harper (1931–2010), the most prominent British charismatic and founder of Fountain Trust; Ralph Wilkerson (b. 1927), founder of Melodyland Christian Center, Anaheim, California; and "Pat" Robertson (b. 1930), founder of the Christian Broadcasting Network and "The 700 Club." The movement seemed to lose much of its forward momentum in the 1980s as related to its influence in the traditional denominations.

A unique feature of the Renewalist Movement was the impact it sustained in the Roman Catholic community. The turmoil in the church that precipitated the calling of Vatican II was the context. In the official literature before the council, loyal Roman Catholics were asked to pray for a new "Pentecost," a renewal.

### Catholic Charismatics

Through various books and contact with the Pentecostal Movement, a group met for what is now called the Duquesne Weekend (1967). There, several experienced the renewing power of the Pentecostal experience within the flexibility of Roman Catholic orthodoxy. The movement spread rapidly across the United States with huge conclaves of priests and laity attending. In the 1970s, it reached the Vatican itself. The characteristics of the Roman Catholic Charismatic Movement are often similar to its Protestant counterpart: the small group setting, Bible study with a facilitator, and less insistence on particular gifts of the Spirit.

### The Third Wave

In the 1990s the Charismatic Movement entered a new phase, sometimes called the Third Wave. It is characterized by a multiplicity of separate movements and emphases. Often, if not always, it can be seen through the media networks of the nation. Curses Theology was popular in the early 1990s. Popularized by James Robinson (b. 1943), it was an exorcist movement that suggested a generational cause for any number of maladies. Prosperity Movement advocates, such as Kenneth (b. 1937) and Gloria Copeland, argue that Christians rightly related to the Spirit have the promise of never being poor or sick unless they lack faith and fall into sin. The Positive Confessional or Word of Faith Movement affirms that the blessing of God's promises depends on the constancy and potency of human faith binding God. It has been called "the name it, claim it movement." Equally intriguing is Kingdom Theology in which advocates conduct prayer marches against territorial demons, reclaiming the ground lost to the Devil. Others argue that the church is on the brink of great success because the primitive pattern of the church has been restored in the fivefold ministry of "apostles, prophets, evangelists, pastors, and teachers" (see Eph. 4:11). The emergence of the Kansas City Prophetical Movement; the Toronto Revival, characterized in part by holy laughter; and the Brownsville Revival are the latest in a seemingly endless array of charismatic experiences and postulations.

### The Vineyard Movement

Of all the new faces the "Third Wave" or Latter Day Restoration Movement has had, few have had the durative and stabilizing effect of the Vineyard Movement, one of the few newer movements to become a denomination. The movement is not unique in its general charismatic openness, but its low-sell approach in these matters and attempts at biblical authenticity have proven attractive. It has been able to draw many into its orbit from traditionally noncharismatic orientations. Founded as an organization in 1982, it now claims several hundred churches. John Wimber (1934–1998), the founder, believed that the charismatic phenomena of the first century should be duplicated in the twentieth, particularly the observation that conversions often followed the working of miracles. This he called "Power Evangelism."

The contribution of the Charismatic Movement has been enormous. Many have found deep spiritual significance through the teachings and a vitality that has given hope and direction. It has produced a huge proliferation of international missionary activity. The impact on the noncharismatic church has largely been in worship style and music.

# The Fortunes of Roman Catholicism

As the importance of religion has experienced eclipse in the public square progressively through the intellectual assault of the Enlightenment on ancient authority sources, the rise of the postmodern spirit has only deepened the tragedy. For any religious tradition that based authority on Scripture, tradition, reason, and experience (in this instance papal infallibility also), the struggles have been significant. Roman Catholicism, like conservative Protestantism, has sought to remain important in people's lives through wise compromises, but theological integrity has often been eclipsed. Additionally, moral dereliction on the part of some in the church's leadership has left it staggering under the threat of litigation and loss of confidence.

In the nineteenth century, the Roman Catholic Church responded to intellectual and political threats by pontifical pronouncements, such as the Syllabus of Errors (1864), which had the effect of driving dissent underground. In the pontificate of Pius IX (1845–1878), Vatican I determined to invest in the church's highest office the ability to speak incontrovertible truth. The pope was given the authority to validate or invalidate all councilor decisions. Pius's solution to liberal trends was an authoritarian suppression of it.

### Inconsistent popes

Between Vatican I (1870) and Vatican II (1963), the popes were not consistent in dealing with the progressive element in the church, who were mostly teachers and low-level administrators. Leo III appears to have been a conciliatory pope (1878–1903), not addressing issues of doctrine nor appealing to papal infallibility to quell dissidents. Pius X (1903–1914) returned to the stern ways of Pius IX, issuing a "New Syllabus of Errors" (1907). The Great War dominated the pontificate of Benedict XV (1914–1922). Pius XI (1922–1939) is best known for his encyclical against birth control in 1930 (*Casti Connubi*). Pius XII (1939–1958), unlike popes since Pius X, pressed his high position to defend traditional teachings. Sadly anti-Semitic during the Second World War, he did exercise his authority within his official capacity to declare the dogma of the Immaculate Assumption of Mary (1950)—that she was translated to heaven apart from death (in 1854 Pius IX pronounced the Immaculate Conception of Mary, that she was conceived apart from the stain of original sin). Cardinal Angelo Giuseppe Roncali, John XXIII (1958–1963), was a progressive pope. He acknowledged past anti-Semitism in the church, though denied by some, sought to make bridges to Islam, and suggested that salvation was possible for atheists and agnostics. He called for a reforming council, Vatican II (1963–1965). His death after the initial session prevented the actualization of many of the reforms for which he had hoped.

Paul VI (1963–1978), a traditionalist, was elected to the highest post two weeks after John's death and inherited a council intending to heal the rising division in the church between progressives and traditionalists by addressing issues of theology and practice. When it became clear that any decisions of the council would be subject to affirmation by the curia, substantive doctrinal changes were unlikely.

### Catholic dialogue

This does not mean there were not changes. An openness for dialogue prevailed in the council toward Protestants. Further, the pope met with the patriarch of the Greek Orthodox Church in the context of a trip to the Holy Land in 1965

**Pope Leo XIII (1810–1903).**

Pope John Paul II (1978–2005), "a kind of Catholic Gorbachev."

rescinding the excommunication that divided them. The council documents affirmed that constituents of churches outside the Roman Catholic community, though seriously defective, should be recognized as "separated brethren." Openness to the emerging charismatic movement through a renewed awareness of the gifts of the Spirit was also evident in the council's findings. On the popular level the laity was given more opportunities to participate as leaders in ministries within the church, meatless Fridays were no longer obligatory, St. Christopher disappeared, a new translation of the Scriptures was authorized (the Confraternity edition), and worship services were made more accessible with the use of vernacular languages. At a more substantive level, that of church dogma, there were no changes, to the chagrin of the progressives. Supreme authority in the church remained in the College of Cardinals who can only act with the sanction of the head of the church. Further, sources of truth remained the Scripture and tradition, the curia and pope being the final arbiters of interpretation. The understanding that sacerdotalism is the means of divine grace were untouched, as was the restriction of the priesthood to celibate males, the rejection of birth control, and the condemnation of abortion. In 1967 Paul VI affirmed the celibacy of the priesthood in *Sacerdotalis Coelibatus*, and in 1968 he condemned artificial means of contraception (*Humanae Vitae*).

**John Paul II**

After the very brief pontificate of John Paul I (1978), John Paul II (1978–2005) began a long ministry as head of the Roman Church. Progressives found him uncongenial to their agenda. Hans Kung, a Roman Catholic renegade, called him a "Catholic Gorbachev" and a "kind of living cult figure." Though he fashioned himself as a John XXIII, some think that he was more like Pius XII. Among his accomplishments was an attempt to reinforce traditional teachings in the church with the publication of *The Catechism of the Catholic Church* (1994). Though touted as a reflection of a shift away from traditional dogmatism, the document is often unclear in crucial areas of difference with traditional Protestantism, and unchanging in such vital areas as the role of the sacraments, purgatory, the role of Mary and the saints, indulgences, and the relationship of Scripture and tradition. In 2000, he beatified Pius IX, the pope who called Vatican I and that declared the dogma of papal infallibility, produced the Syllabus of Error to suppress progressives, and declared the Immaculate Conception of Mary. The recent document, *Evangelical and Catholics Together: The Christian Mission in the Third Millennium* has sparked another round of Roman Catholic–Protestant dialogue. That Protestants would be enamored with the possibility of doctrinal change in Rome is more suggestive of the weakening of Protestants than a softening of Roman Catholicism.

**Benedict XVI**

The new century witnessed the appointment of Joseph Cardinal Ratzinger as Benedict XVI (2005). A confidante of John Paul II, he inherited a diverse and troubled church, as much so as the Protestant communities. Youth attendance in the Roman Church has declined by two-thirds, and candidates for the priesthood have declined by 50 percent, so that church posts are left vacant. The laity of the church favor the marriage of priests (87%) and approve of the ordination of women (67%). A significant majority of the laity favor the admission of the divorced to communion (74%), favor some allowance for abortion (85%), and believe that one can contradict church teachings and be a good Roman Catholic (81%). The Roman Church appears to be in a momentous free fall as the hierarchy desperately seeks ways to prevent it.

# The Unification Movements

Within Christendom a current has existed for centuries seeking to accomplish common goals through the pursuit of mutual cooperation. The fracturing of Christendom with the Reformation has brought certain urgency to such endeavors. However, factors that emerged two centuries ago catapulted the impetus into national and international prominence.

**Ecumenical origins**

The origins of the modern ecumenical movement are in nineteenth-century interdenominational missionary enterprise, springing from the Second Great Awakening in the United States (the American Bible Society [1816], the American Sunday School Union [1824]) and in England (YMCA [1844], the Evangelical Alliance [1846], and Salvation Army [1865]).

Efforts to effect a closer unity among the churches, an intradenominational coalition, were proposed by several in the nineteenth century. Samuel Schmucker (1799–1873), founder of Luther Theological Seminary, Gettysburg, Pennsylvania (1825), organized the American branch of the Evangelical Alliance (1846). Philip Schaff (1819–1893), the celebrated church historian, spoke in his inaugural address (1844) at the German Reformed Seminary in Mercersburg, Pennsylvania, of his hope for a reunion of Christendom, ending the schism occasioned by the sixteenth-century Reformation.

**Federal Council of Churches**

The cooperative sentiment evident in the nineteenth century led in the United States to the founding of the Federal Council of Churches in 1908, restructured in 1950 as the National Council of Churches. The makeup of the FCC, as well as the distinctively social agenda of the organization, made most conservatives leery. The FCC began with some twenty-nine denominational bodies forming several commissions to structure their efforts. Among the early leaders in the council were Shailer Mathews (1863–1941), president and prominent leader in the growing liberal wing of the Baptist churches; Walter Rauschenbusch (1861–1918), prominent in the social gospel movement; and John R. Mott (1865–1955), an advocate of its missions efforts. The National Council of Churches, USA, claims to speak for 100,000 churches in some thirty-five denominations with a total constituency of over forty-five million (approximately 16.6% of the national population). Affiliates in the NCC include the traditional mainline denominations (excluding the Southern Baptist Convention and the Lutheran Church, Missouri Synod), several Orthodox communities, and African-American denominations. In addition, the NCC works with some fifty unaffiliated faith groups, such as the Roman Catholic Church, in common endeavors. Conceiving the Great Commission as primarily care for the plight of the disadvantaged, the NCC is strident in its promotion of minority and human rights, world peace, the ending of world hunger, health services (sometimes with left-wing political advocacy), and many other humanitarian endeavors. The NCC maintains fraternal relations with the World Council of Churches, but is not organically connected to it.

**Churches in Christ Uniting**

The ecumenical enterprise entered a new phase in the 1960s with the proposal of Eugene Carson Blake, stated clerk of the United Presbyterian Church, for an organic unification of the American churches. Nine denominations (among them the AME; the AMEZ; the Episcopal Church; the Presbyterian Church, USA; the United Church of Christ; and the United Methodist Church) joined in the initial dream birthed in 1962, the Consultation Church Union (COCU). In 2002 the enterprise was reborn after decades of inertia with the creation of Churches in Christ Uniting (CICU). In what

**The inaugural meeting of the World Council of Churches in Amsterdam, August 1948.**

appears to be classic postmodern posturing, the participating denominations agreed to create an organization where diversity can be celebrated in unity.

Like the NCC, the World Council of Churches (1948) has roots in the nineteen-century cooperative missions movement. As the leading Christian ecumenical organization, it boasts of some 348 churches or denominations in 120 countries with a combined constituency of 550 million. It claims in its membership the vast majority of the Orthodox communities, the worldwide Anglican Communion, and most of the mainline Protestant denominations. (The Roman Catholic Church is not a member, but it has worked closely with the WCC for three decades.) In its humanitarian and political values, the WCC parallels the United Nations' humanitarian efforts.

**Roots of the WCC**

The roots of the WCC can be traced to the creation of the Edinburgh International Missionary Council (1910), though this organization did not join the WCC until 1961. The actual creation of the WCC in 1948 came with the merger of the Faith and Order Movement, established in 1927 by Charles Brent (1862–1929), and the Life and Work Movement, established by Nathan Soderblum (1866–1931) in 1925. After several meetings to discuss a formal union of efforts and delays brought on by a global conflict, 147 denominations from 44 countries gathered at Amsterdam for the first meeting of the World Council of Churches (1948). In 1971 the World Council of Christian Education (1907) joined the WCC. The organization meets about every seven years, the gathering in 2006 having been in Port Alegre, Brazil.

Because of the diversity of theologies as well as much of the social-political agenda represented in both the NCC and the WCC, the conservative wings of Protestantism view them with suspicion. Without eschewing the importance of Christian unity or of compassion for the poor, many feel that union should not come at the expense of historic orthodox conceptions of faith, duties, or priorities. Members of these orthodox communities are involved in numerous expressions of compassion, such as World Vision, and desire to pursue the unity of the body of Christ. Affiliation with the NCC or the WCC, they believe, would seriously compromise the overall task of the Christian church.

# Third World Faith: The Emerging Churches

By the estimate of many sociologists of religion, Christianity is in a state of decline in the West. The religious apathy in the western industrialized nations has reached epidemic proportions. This, however, presents a distorted image of the overall impact of Christianity. Though nations that once were vibrantly pulsating with the values and passions of true Christian faith are now experiencing severe declines in church attendance and have become mission fields, in other parts of the world the church is experiencing unprecedented growth.

The locus of Christian presence has migrated over the centuries. In the first millennium after Christ the population center was Asia and North Africa. In a good portion of the second millennium, particularly with the reformation movements of the sixteenth century and subsequent missions activity, the locus was centered in Western Europe and, later, North America. For example, in the beginning of the nineteenth century only 1 percent of the professing Christian world could be identified outside Europe and North America. The figure was 10 percent by 1900 and 66 percent by 2000.

**New Christian centers**

In this new century, missiologists indicate that the new population centers of Christianity will be below the equator in South America and Africa, as well as in the Pacific Rim nations and China. In those places Christianity is burgeoning. The World Christian Encyclopedia (2001 ed.) indicates

# Christianity in Latin America

**Meeting of the International Missionary Council at Tambaram, Madras, India in 1938, forerunner of the World Council of Churches.**

that the net increase of new converts on the African Continent is 1.5 million annually, over 4,100 daily. The weakening of the superpowers after the end of World War II brought an end to the era of European colonialism, and the "Third World" emerged. Carved from the British empire were Pakistan and India in 1947; from Dutch colonialism, Indonesia; the French relinquished Indo-China in 1954, creating Vietnam, Laos, and Cambodia; and from the former French holdings also came Algeria (1962). In 1957 Ghana became the first African nation to emerge from the yoke of British colonialism. Nigeria followed in 1960 and Kenya in 1963. Germany relinquished Tanzania to Great Britain and it was granted independence in 1961. Zaire gained independence in 1961 from Belgium. The Soviet empire in Central Asia ended with the collapse of the USSR in 1991, the last vestige of European colonialism.

Though the United States will continue through the current century to have the largest number of professing Christians of any nation in the world, Brazil and Mexico will rank second and third by 2050 (195 and 145 million respectively). Nigeria, Zaire, and Ethiopia will rank fifth, sixth, and seventh (145 million, 123 million, and 121 million respectively). Missiologists estimate that by 2050 Russia will have 80 million claiming the Christian faith and China 60 million.

Christianity at century's end will look vastly different. Instead of being white, it will be predominately black, brown, and Asian. Probably it will not be so deeply shaped by western rationalism as it has for the past several centuries.

# The Civil Rights Movement

One of the most important religious/secular movements in recent decades in the United States has been the move to make equality the possession of every citizen. The struggle for equal access for all gave the nation new heroes, from the conservative, nonviolent measures of Martin Luther King Jr. (1929–1968) to the radicalism of Malcolm X (1925–1965), the Black Panthers (founded by Huey Newton [1942–1989] and Bobby Seale [b. 1936] in 1966), and Louis Farrakhan (b. 1934), leader of the Nation of Islam.

**The "third revolution"**

The Civil Rights Movement of the 1950s to 1970s has been described as the nation's "third revolution." The American Revolution applied in principle the notion of equality. The Civil War amendments to the Constitution (14–16) stated it as the right of all citizens, but it did not become a reality until recent decades. The Civil Rights Movement aimed at desegregating public places, from buses to schools to restaurants. Rosa Parks (1913–2005), reeling from the murder of Emmett Till some days earlier, refused to relinquish her seat on a public bus, precipitating the Montgomery, Alabama, bus boycott (1955–1956). In 1957, Central High School, Little Rock, Arkansas, was forcibly integrated. The Washington, D.C., march of over a quarter of a million heard Dr. King deliver the rallying cry of the movement, "I have a dream," on August 28, 1963. The following year the Civil Rights Act was passed, guaranteeing freedom for all. To assure the perpetuation of their gains, the NAACP, the Southern Christian Leadership Conference, and King pushed for the registration of black voters. This led to the Voting Rights Act of 1965, the single most important legislation of the civil rights movement. It assured that no one would be denied access to voting privilege because of race or color.

The Civil Rights Movement, and its supporting organizations, has weakened since the 1970s. This has come about, in part, from the accomplishment of its goals but also because of division in its ranks. King broadened his interests to the peace movement during the Vietnam era, and his murder in Memphis, Tennessee, deprived the movement of his strength.

A meeting of a Ku Klux Klan (KKK) chapter in 1920s USA. The Klan advocated white supremacy and violently oppressed African Americans, Jews, and Roman Catholics.

# The "World" of Postmodernity, Religion, and Ethics

The decline of secular rationalism (brought about by disillusionment with its promises of a better, safer tomorrow through the promotion of education and technology) has created a void—despite enormous physical improvements in almost every field—that does not seem to be filled by economic prosperity, recreational diversions, or the decline of moral restraints. While the Enlightenment disparaged the past and its rich, helpful traditions for an "all-things-new" approach, the inherent assumption of the makers of the modern era was that the most important things in life are physical and material. In effect, the modern era shunned or sadly disfigured the world of immateriality, and that has left western humankind empty of meaning in any deep spiritual sense. The incessant diminution of the role of historic religion has come at a huge cost: the loss of human meaning and hope.

### Secularization

The fact that humans cannot live without a sense of transcendence has led not to the extinction of religion, but to the perversion of it. In the 1960s and 1970s, the rejection of traditional religion for a secularized version of it became evident in secular humanism. It was the complete elevation of man in all his emptiness. God was declared to be nonexistent. He was banished from the earth, and religion was reduced to superstition. The human species was a product of blind evolutionary force, there was no progress in history, right and wrong were situational, and death would bring nonexistence. Humankind's savior was himself.

Secular humanism was the child of the explosive 1960s. Though popular on the college scene, it lacked answers for life's disappointments. Somehow there was a need for more than reasonable explanations.

### The New Age

A more recent, largely failed attempt to find meaning has been the enormously popular—at least in the publishing industry and bookstores—New Age Movement. Unlike its earlier counterpart, it recognized the reality of a nonmaterial world of spirit and consciousness, a world without death but only reincarnation. It was the influx of vestiges of eastern religions and the occult. Though humankind was viewed as a spiritual being, personal progress was dependent on grasping the significance of personal, internal strengths. The conscious self replaced reason and technology in problem solving. Ethics were a matter of personal preference. Values clarification was the insight, often taught in the public schools, that there are few absolute values. All religious opinions are equally valuable; intolerance, the great sin of postmodern culture, is not socially acceptable. "Political correctness" is contrary to historic Christian orthodoxy with its nonallowance for false truth claims.

**Grotesque "Day of Death" figurines. Syncretistic and New Age religions have proliferated since the mid twentieth century.**

# What's Next?

In the past century, prognosticators seemed to come to rather bleak conclusions. Aldous Huxley (1894–1963), the British novelist, wrote of the dangers of biological, chemical, and psychological engineering as tools of statecraft (*Brave New World* [1931]). In *Brave New World Revisited* (1958), his fears were more intense and he sought social sanity in the controlled use of drugs such as LSD. It seemed that there was no hope. In 1944 George Orwell published *Animal Farm* as an anti-Stalinist allegory, fearing the rise of global Communism. This was followed five years later by *1984*. For Orwell, like Huxley, the future was dark. Totalitarianism threatened the world. However, not all writers were so overwhelmingly pessimistic. Alvin Toffler (b. 1928), a futurologist, has argued that the current cultural crisis is the result of a shift from the industrial age (1700) to the information age—the computer age (1956). He suggested in *The Third Wave* (New York: Morrow, 1980) that times of transition lead to momentary disorientation, and humankind needs to suffer through this one. A better time, a more psychologically wholesome era, is about to burst on the scene.

**The church of the Savior is on an uninterrupted march through the centuries.**

**What of the future?**
The Christian perspective is vastly different from that of any of these writers. The future does not contain the world envisioned by Huxley or Orwell. Dangers will come and go, but the invisible hand of Almighty God is potently active restraining evil and promoting His kingdom in the affairs of humankind. The church will endure persecution and the gospel will continue to be proclaimed throughout the world. The church will continue to prosper until the God of heaven brings an end to this temporal sphere in fiery judgment, and the kingdoms of this world become the kingdom of God's dear Son. As Toffler has indicated, the world is in chaos and change; it is a disorienting time. However, the chaos will not end in a peaceful reconciliation with the latest computer technology. Humankind will not bring about the peace that they crave. Though progress is certainly possible, there will always be a circumstance, a movement, a person to remind everyone that the best of things is only a temporary shadow of permanence beyond social engineering.

So what's next? The answer seems to be more of the same—more pain, more successes, more wonderful triumphs, more delights, more disappointments. The church of the Savior is on an uninterrupted march through the centuries to its final triumphant consummation. When that will be, no one knows. What we do know and should seek to implement is what Jesus instructed us: we are to love the Lord God with all the faculties of our being and express that in love for our neighbors!

# Index